A YEAR OF INTUITIVE TAROT

2023
WEEKLY PLANNER
JULY 2022–DECEMBER 2023

2023 YEAR AT A GLANCE

JANUARY

S	M	T	W	T	F	S
1	2	3	4	5	6	7
8	9	10	11	12	13	14
15	16	17	18	19	20	21
22	23	24	25	26	27	28
29	30	31				

FEBRUARY

S	M	T	W	T	F	S
			1	2	3	4
5	6	7	8	9	10	11
12	13	14	15	16	17	18
19	20	21	22	23	24	25
26	27	28				

MARCH

S	M	T	W	T	F	S
			1	2	3	4
5	6	7	8	9	10	11
12	13	14	15	16	17	18
19	20	21	22	23	24	25
26	27	28	29	30	31	

APRIL

S	M	T	W	T	F	S
						1
2	3	4	5	6	7	8
9	10	11	12	13	14	15
16	17	18	19	20	21	22
23	24	25	26	27	28	29
30						

MAY

S	M	T	W	T	F	S
	1	2	3	4	5	6
7	8	9	10	11	12	13
14	15	16	17	18	19	20
21	22	23	24	25	26	27
28	29	30	31			

JUNE

S	M	T	W	T	F	S
				1	2	3
4	5	6	7	8	9	10
11	12	13	14	15	16	17
18	19	20	21	22	23	24
25	26	27	28	29	30	

JULY

S	M	T	W	T	F	S
						1
2	3	4	5	6	7	8
9	10	11	12	13	14	15
16	17	18	19	20	21	22
23	24	25	26	27	28	29
30	31					

AUGUST

S	M	T	W	T	F	S
		1	2	3	4	5
6	7	8	9	10	11	12
13	14	15	16	17	18	19
20	21	22	23	24	25	26
27	28	29	30	31		

SEPTEMBER

S	M	T	W	T	F	S
					1	2
3	4	5	6	7	8	9
10	11	12	13	14	15	16
17	18	19	20	21	22	23
24	25	26	27	28	29	30

OCTOBER

S	M	T	W	T	F	S
1	2	3	4	5	6	7
8	9	10	11	12	13	14
15	16	17	18	19	20	21
22	23	24	25	26	27	28
29	30	31				

NOVEMBER

S	M	T	W	T	F	S
			1	2	3	4
5	6	7	8	9	10	11
12	13	14	15	16	17	18
19	20	21	22	23	24	25
26	27	28	29	30		

DECEMBER

S	M	T	W	T	F	S
					1	2
3	4	5	6	7	8	9
10	11	12	13	14	15	16
17	18	19	20	21	22	23
24	25	26	27	28	29	30
31						

2024 YEAR AT A GLANCE

JANUARY

S	M	T	W	T	F	S
	1	2	3	4	5	6
7	8	9	10	11	12	13
14	15	16	17	18	19	20
21	22	23	24	25	26	27
28	29	30	31			

FEBRUARY

S	M	T	W	T	F	S
				1	2	3
4	5	6	7	8	9	10
11	12	13	14	15	16	17
18	19	20	21	22	23	24
25	26	27	28	29		

MARCH

S	M	T	W	T	F	S
					1	2
3	4	5	6	7	8	9
10	11	12	13	14	15	16
17	18	19	20	21	22	23
24	25	26	27	28	29	30
31						

APRIL

S	M	T	W	T	F	S
	1	2	3	4	5	6
7	8	9	10	11	12	13
14	15	16	17	18	19	20
21	22	23	24	25	26	27
28	29	30				

MAY

S	M	T	W	T	F	S
			1	2	3	4
5	6	7	8	9	10	11
12	13	14	15	16	17	18
19	20	21	22	23	24	25
26	27	28	29	30	31	

JUNE

S	M	T	W	T	F	S
						1
2	3	4	5	6	7	8
9	10	11	12	13	14	15
16	17	18	19	20	21	22
23	24	25	26	27	28	29
30						

JULY

S	M	T	W	T	F	S
	1	2	3	4	5	6
7	8	9	10	11	12	13
14	15	16	17	18	19	20
21	22	23	24	25	26	27
28	29	30	31			

AUGUST

S	M	T	W	T	F	S
				1	2	3
4	5	6	7	8	9	10
11	12	13	14	15	16	17
18	19	20	21	22	23	24
25	26	27	28	29	30	31

SEPTEMBER

S	M	T	W	T	F	S
1	2	3	4	5	6	7
8	9	10	11	12	13	14
15	16	17	18	19	20	21
22	23	24	25	26	27	28
29	30					

OCTOBER

S	M	T	W	T	F	S
		1	2	3	4	5
6	7	8	9	10	11	12
13	14	15	16	17	18	19
20	21	22	23	24	25	26
27	28	29	30	31		

NOVEMBER

S	M	T	W	T	F	S
					1	2
3	4	5	6	7	8	9
10	11	12	13	14	15	16
17	18	19	20	21	22	23
24	25	26	27	28	29	30

DECEMBER

S	M	T	W	T	F	S
1	2	3	4	5	6	7
8	9	10	11	12	13	14
15	16	17	18	19	20	21
22	23	24	25	26	27	28
29	30	31				

The tarot uncovers our greatest strengths and our deepest secrets. It acts as a mirror to our soul, reflecting back to us precisely what we need to continue growing into the best versions of ourselves. We can gain divine wisdom about ourselves and our lives by merely understanding the stories within the tarot.

The 22 Major Arcana cards will more often concern deeper, more life-impacting matters. Although they can be read for their individual meanings, they can also be seen as part of a larger, even mythic journey. The 56 Minor Arcana cards do not deal with quite the same level of life-altering situations as the Major Arcana. They deal with money, decision-making, and relationships, just to name a few topics of interest.

In addition to scheduling your time, you can use this planner alongside your personal deck to create a three-card spread to start off each month. This spread will guide you on which areas of your life require your focus, what might be holding you back, and what possibilities are in store for you.

In reading your monthly spreads, you will be weaving together the story, symbols, and meanings of the cards in front of you with the addition of connecting to a source greater than yourself to gain insights into the future of your month and how to make the most of each throughout the year.

JULY 2022

NOTES	SUNDAY	MONDAY	TUESDAY
	3	4	5
		INDEPENDENCE DAY (US)	
	10	11	12
	17	18	19
	24	25	26
	31		

JULY 2022

WEDNESDAY	THURSDAY	FRIDAY	SATURDAY
		1 CANADA DAY (CAN)	2
6	7	8	9
13	14	15	16
20	21	22	23
27	28	29	30

The tarot acts as a potent self-discovery system that has the power to catapult you into the farthest reaches of your soul.

MONDAY (JUNE)	27

TUESDAY (JUNE)	28

WEDNESDAY (JUNE)	29

THURSDAY (JUNE)	30

FRIDAY (CANADA DAY ((AN)	1

SATURDAY	2

SUNDAY	3

JULY 2022

MONDAY
INDEPENDENCE DAY (US)

4

TUESDAY

5

WEDNESDAY

6

THURSDAY ◖

7

FRIDAY   8

SATURDAY   9

SUNDAY   10

QUEEN OF PENTACLES
Here's a secret: Nurturing is hard
work! Are you taking care of others
or are you too busy taking care
of yourself? Maybe things need
rebalancing. Security can come at a
price but it is usually worth it.

QUEEN OF PENTACLES

JULY 2022

MONDAY   11

TUESDAY   12

WEDNESDAY ●   13

THURSDAY   14

FRIDAY 15

SATURDAY 16

SUNDAY 17

ACE OF WANDS
This is a good time to ponder the well of your inspiration. Do you have a deep and underlying passion? If so, now might be the time to follow it. Conditions may be well-suited for creation, invention, and even rebirth.

JULY 2022

MONDAY   18

TUESDAY   19

WEDNESDAY ☽   20

THURSDAY   21

FRIDAY

22

SATURDAY

23

SUNDAY

24

TWO OF CUPS
Two can be stronger than one.
Harmony and partnership trumps
disunity. A romance could be
waiting, or a new friendship. They
might be coming to you or you could
have to go looking. Keep your eyes
and heart open.

TWO OF CUPS

JULY 2022

MONDAY   25

TUESDAY   26

WEDNESDAY   27

THURSDAY ○   28

FRIDAY

29

SATURDAY

30

SUNDAY

31

PAGE OF SWORDS

Focus and direction may not be your strong suit at the moment. New ideas, possibilities, dreams, and desires keep your head buzzing. You can try to harness that flow or follow it where it takes you.

AUGUST

THE WORLD

Your long journey is coming to an end. As you walk through one phase into the next, it's time to honor and celebrate how far you've come and how much you've integrated. Though your expansion will never end, you've come to an important moment of culmination. The World card rolls into your life to honor and celebrate a time of fulfillment in your journey. You will likely attain a goal you've been working toward, either externally or internally. All four elements are associated with this card to represent your mastery and offer you safe passage as you move through to a new journey. The World is governed by the planet Saturn, the wise ruler of the sky that honors structure and discipline. The message of Saturn's energy is clear: As long as you're a physical being, you'll be ruled by the elements.

THE WORLD REVERSED

When the reversed World appears, it indicates that the closure you're seeking may be withheld at the moment. This withholding could be internal or external in source. It will be important for you to assess and determine the source of the pause in your journey. Maybe you're intentionally sabotaging your growth for fear of success, or you have a belief that you don't deserve to be rewarded. This reversed card could also indicate a need to fine-tune something on your path, as you're not quite ready to come to the end of this journey.

CARD 1

My focus for the month.

CARD 2

Roadblocks I need to overcome this month.

CARD 3

Possibilities that are in store for me this month.

What does this spread make me feel?

My takeaway for the month:

AUGUST 2022

NOTES	SUNDAY	MONDAY	TUESDAY
		1 SUMMER BANK HOLIDAY (UK-SCT)	2
	7	8	9
	14	15	16
	21	22	23
	28	29 SUMMER BANK HOLIDAY (UK-ENG / NIR / WAL)	30

AUGUST 2022

WEDNESDAY	THURSDAY	FRIDAY	SATURDAY
3	4	5	6
10	11	12	13
17	18	19	20
24	25	26	27
31			

Reflect on your journey of the last year
and prepare yourself to look ahead.
Allow time to celebrate your new journey.
Cook a nourishing meal, dance to the
music, prepare for a fresh start while being
grateful for how far you've come.

MONDAY
SUMMER BANK HOLIDAY (UK-SCT)

1

TUESDAY

2

WEDNESDAY

3

THURSDAY

4

FRIDAY ◖

5

SATURDAY

6

SUNDAY

7

AUGUST 2022

MONDAY 8

TUESDAY 9

WEDNESDAY 10

THURSDAY ● 11

FRIDAY

12

SATURDAY

13

SUNDAY

14

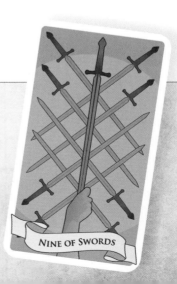

NINE OF SWORDS
There is no limit to things that you can
be worried about. Some can be real, but
others may be just phantoms, anxieties,
or figments of your imagination. Separate
the real from the imagined.

AUGUST 2022

MONDAY 15

TUESDAY 16

WEDNESDAY 17

THURSDAY 18

FRIDAY ◗   19

SATURDAY   20

SUNDAY   21

KING OF SWORDS
Being in charge can be as simple as just
thinking it. Use that confidence to be decisive.
Keep your standards high. Do not settle
for second best. But do not forget to show
compassion as well.

AUGUST 2022

MONDAY   22

TUESDAY   23

WEDNESDAY   24

THURSDAY   25

FRIDAY

26

SATURDAY ○

27

SUNDAY

28

FOUR OF WANDS

You have been on a journey and undergone significant change. It could be time for you to rest and recuperate. Find your place of refuge, whether with yourself or with beloved others. Consider how far you have come.

SEPTEMBER

THE FOOL

THE FOOL

The energy of The Fool is one of pure openness and wonder. This card calls to the childlike nature of your spirit. You're walking forward, arms outstretched, with stars in your eyes, and don't have a care in the world. This card is calling you to fully embody the energy of The Fool. Perhaps you already have the internal whispers of this sensation about a new journey. Alternatively, this card may be calling you to find a sense of wonderment and openness in an area of your life. The Fool's journey is not always one of joy and cheer, but The Fool doesn't care. The Fool's ability to walk into any situation with an inquisitive mind and heart is the true nature of this card. Can you find ways to embody the energy as you embark on new adventures, even if you know the path ahead may be rocky?

THE FOOL REVERSED

The reversed energy of The Fool indicates an unwillingness to move ahead or a feeling of being stuck. You may be in a forced state of stagnation, too afraid of what might lie ahead. Remember, life is a mixed bag of joy, and you came here to grow. Alternatively, this card reversed could show that you're being dangerously naive. Can you find ways to balance your desire for change and growth before floating off into the unknown?

CARD 1
My focus for the month.

CARD 2
Roadblocks I need to overcome this month.

CARD 3
Possibilities that are in store for me this month.

What does this spread make me feel?

My takeaway for the month:

SEPTEMBER 2022

NOTES	SUNDAY	MONDAY	TUESDAY
	4	5	6
	FATHER'S DAY (AUS / NZ)	LABOR DAY (US) LABOUR DAY (CAN)	
	11	12	13
	PATRIOT DAY (US) GRANDPARENTS' DAY (US)		
	18	19	20
	25	26	27
	ROSH HASHANAH (BEGINS AT SUNDOWN)		

SEPTEMBER 2022

WEDNESDAY	THURSDAY	FRIDAY	SATURDAY
	1	2	3
7	8	9	10
14	15 FIRST DAY OF NATIONAL HISPANIC HERITAGE MONTH	16	17
21	22 FALL EQUINOX	23	24
28	29	30	

Start a new project, meditate with the intent to be open to new ideas, perform a New Moon ritual, sing, or express yourself through writing or speaking.

AUGUST/SEPTEMBER 2022

MONDAY (AUGUST)
SUMMER BANK HOLIDAY (UK-ENG / NIR / WAL)
29

TUESDAY (AUGUST)
30

WEDNESDAY (AUGUST)
31

THURSDAY
1

FRIDAY
2

SATURDAY
3

SUNDAY
FATHER'S DAY (AUS / NZ)
4

SEPTEMBER 2022

MONDAY
LABOR DAY (US) / LABOUR DAY (CAN)

5

TUESDAY

6

WEDNESDAY

7

THURSDAY

8

FRIDAY   9

_____

SATURDAY ●   10

_____

SUNDAY   11
PATRIOT DAY (US) / GRANDPARENTS' DAY (US)

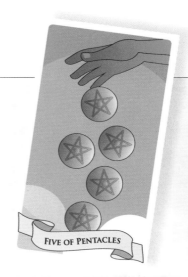

FIVE OF PENTACLES
Try as you might, not everything
comes up roses. When you hit a bad
patch, remind yourself that help can
usually be found. You just need to look
around you.

FIVE OF PENTACLES

SEPTEMBER 2022

MONDAY 12

TUESDAY 13

WEDNESDAY 14

THURSDAY 15

NATIONAL HISPANIC HERITAGE MONTH BEGINS

FRIDAY   16

SATURDAY 🌓   17

SUNDAY   18

KNIGHT OF CUPS
New possibilities could be headed
your way. Romance, adventure, some
long-desired opportunity. Be relaxed
but prepared. Who knows what form
the messenger could take or whether
you will hear the message?

SEPTEMBER 2022

MONDAY 19

TUESDAY 20

WEDNESDAY 21

THURSDAY 22
FALL EQUINOX

FRIDAY   23

SATURDAY   24

SUNDAY ○   25
ROSH HASHANAH (BEGINS AT SUNDOWN)

EIGHT OF SWORDS
Some traps we set ourselves. The good
news is that those can be the easier
ones to deal with once you find them.
Be vigilant.

OCTOBER

THE MAGICIAN

THE MAGICIAN

The Magician embodies all four elements: earth, air, water, and fire. The Magician understands that they have every tool they need at their fingertips and infinite ability to tap into them. This card calls you to notice all of the power you have. How can you make use of your divine gifts and use them for positive change for yourself and others? The energy of this card is one of mastery, willpower, and resourcefulness. The Magician may be calling you to dig deep for the strength and power you need to make powerful changes in your life or the world. This energy is not only about using your resources but also directing them with skill. Ruled by Mercury, The Magician also knows how to communicate clearly to effectively share their knowledge and wisdom with others.

THE MAGICIAN REVERSED

The energy of The Magician reversed could indicate a couple of things. It could mean to show you that you're blinding yourself from all of the tools you have nearby. Have you found yourself stuck with a sense of hopelessness? Can you find ways to work with what you have? Alternatively, this card's energy reversed could indicate that you're overusing your power in harmful ways. Understand that whatever you put out into the world will come back to you eventually.

CARD 1

My focus for the month.

CARD 2

Roadblocks I need to overcome this month.

CARD 3

Possibilities that are in store for me this month.

What does this spread make me feel?

My takeaway for the month:

OCTOBER 2022

NOTES	SUNDAY	MONDAY	TUESDAY
	◗ 2	3	4 YOM KIPPUR (BEGINS AT SUNDOWN)
	● 9 SUKKOT (BEGINS AT SUNDOWN)	10 INDIGENOUS PEOPLES' DAY (US) (COLUMBUS DAY (US) THANKSGIVING DAY ((AN)	11
	16	◗ 17 SIMCHAT TORAH (BEGINS AT SUNDOWN)	18
	23	24 LABOUR DAY (NZ)	○ 25
	30	31 HALLOWEEN	

OCTOBER 2022

WEDNESDAY	THURSDAY	FRIDAY	SATURDAY
			1
5	6	7	8
12	13	14	15
19	20	21	22
26	27	28	29

Intuition is the voice of the soul.
Listen to it.

SEPTEMBER/OCTOBER 2022

MONDAY (SEPTEMBER)

26

TUESDAY (SEPTEMBER)

27

WEDNESDAY (SEPTEMBER)

28

THURSDAY (SEPTEMBER)

29

FRIDAY (SEPTEMBER)

30

SATURDAY

1

SUNDAY

2

OCTOBER 2022

MONDAY
3

TUESDAY
YOM KIPPUR (BEGINS AT SUNDOWN)
4

WEDNESDAY
5

THURSDAY
6

FRIDAY

7

SATURDAY

8

SUNDAY
SUKKOT (BEGINS AT SUNDOWN)

9

TWO OF PENTACLES
You have a lot going on. How are
you balancing your priorities?
Are you a good enough juggler
or is it time to cut back?

OCTOBER 2022

MONDAY
INDIGENOUS PEOPLES' DAY (US) / COLUMBUS DAY (US) /
THANKSGIVING DAY (CAN)

10

TUESDAY

11

WEDNESDAY

12

THURSDAY

13

FRIDAY

14

SATURDAY

15

SUNDAY

16

FIVE OF CUPS
You could have lost something of importance or faced a trying time with emotional consequences. But keeping your head down makes it hard to see the good that is coming.

OCTOBER 2022

MONDAY ☽

SIMCHAT TORAH (BEGINS AT SUNDOWN)

17

TUESDAY

18

WEDNESDAY

19

THURSDAY

20

FRIDAY

21

SATURDAY

22

SUNDAY

23

TWO OF SWORDS
There are important choices to make about your future. But the way ahead is unclear. You may feel stuck in between. However, you have all the tools you need to make your decision.

OCTOBER 2022

MONDAY
LABOUR DAY (NZ)

24

TUESDAY ○

25

WEDNESDAY

26

THURSDAY

27

FRIDAY   28

SATURDAY   29

SUNDAY   30

DEATH

Something is coming to an end. There
is a chance for rebirth, renewal, and
getting out of old habits. Are you ready
for a new chapter of your life?

DEATH

NOVEMBER

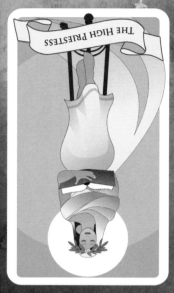

THE HIGH PRIESTESS

The High Priestess is a powerful call for you to connect with the beyond. You came from Source Energy and are always connected to the spirit realm, your guides, and your ancestors. This card is calling you to reconnect with this side. Be open to new ways to connect with Spirit and your natural intuitive gifts. Beyond the spirit realm, the High Priestess also calls you to acknowledge your subconscious. We cannot become one without full integration. Understanding and working with your shadow is a necessary part of becoming whole and honoring the depth of your mystical abilities. Don't shy away from the difficult or scary aspects of your being. Rather, embrace them and hold them closer to heal them. The High Priestess is ruled by the Moon, so this card could also be calling you to connect with Mother Moon in more meaningful ways.

THE HIGH PRIESTESS REVERSED

The High Priestess reversed could indicate that you've cut yourself off from the spirit world and intuitive gifts, either intentionally or unintentionally. If you believe that you don't have intuition or feel as though you can't trust it, it's time to reconsider. If working with your intuition is new to you, you've been initiated, and it's time to start the journey. There may be important information being withheld from you if you're unwilling to receive it.

CARD 1

My focus for the month.

CARD 2

Roadblocks I need to overcome this month.

CARD 3

Possibilities that are in store for me this month.

What does this spread make me feel?

My takeaway for the month:

NOVEMBER 2022

NOTES	SUNDAY	MONDAY	TUESDAY
			◗ 1 ALL SAINTS' DAY
	6 DAYLIGHT SAVING TIME ENDS (US / CAN)	7	● 8 ELECTION DAY (US)
	13	14	15
	20	21	22
	27	28	29

NOVEMBER 2022

WEDNESDAY	THURSDAY	FRIDAY	SATURDAY
2	3	4	5
9	10	11 VETERANS DAY (US)	12
16	17	18	19
23	24 THANKSGIVING DAY (US)	25 NATIVE AMERICAN HERITAGE DAY (US)	26
30			

Light a candle or enjoy a bonfire, play, exercise, pick up a project you put down or write a list of your favorite qualities.

MONDAY (OCTOBER)   31
HALLOWEEN

TUESDAY ◖   1
ALL SAINTS' DAY

WEDNESDAY   2

THURSDAY   3

FRIDAY   4

SATURDAY   5

SUNDAY   6
DAYLIGHT SAVING TIME ENDS (US / CAN)

NOVEMBER 2022

MONDAY
7

TUESDAY ●
ELECTION DAY (US)
8

WEDNESDAY
9

THURSDAY
10

FRIDAY
VETERANS DAY (US)

11

SATURDAY

12

SUNDAY

13

EIGHT OF PENTACLES
You have skills, no doubt. But you can always
be better. Consider yourself an apprentice.
Be dedicated, serious, and sincere. After all,
practice makes perfect.

NOVEMBER 2022

MONDAY
14

TUESDAY
15

WEDNESDAY ☽
16

THURSDAY
17

FRIDAY 18

SATURDAY 19

SUNDAY 20

ACE OF CUPS
This is a time of emotional abundance. New relationships could be starting or older ones revitalized. You could be inspired to make a fresh start. Go with it! (But don't get carried away.)

NOVEMBER 2022

MONDAY 21

TUESDAY 22

WEDNESDAY ○ 23

THURSDAY 24
THANKSGIVING DAY (US)

FRIDAY
NATIVE AMERICAN HERITAGE DAY (US)

25

SATURDAY

26

SUNDAY

27

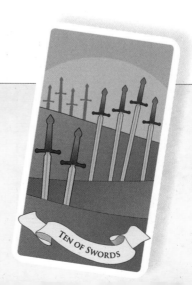

TEN OF SWORDS

Things may look dark. When dealt a serious blow, it can be easy to lose hope. But you are still standing. Now is a time for rebuilding.

DECEMBER

THE EMPRESS

The Empress is the divine mother and supreme caregiver of the tarot. The energy of this card calls you to find deep reverence for nature and your physical vessel. The earth is the ultimate source of life and physical creation and should be honored with great regard. The Empress's energy calls you to find deep joy in physical creation and to birth new projects, ideas, or possibly a child. The Empress is fertile ground for your desires. The Empress is ruled by Venus, the planet of love and attraction. This energy calls you to find ways to honor your body and indulge in the physical senses. This card may also be calling you to bring something new into the world.

THE EMPRESS REVERSED

The Empress reversed is a sign that you've been neglecting your physical body or the world around you. This card can come up if you've been spending too much time in the upper realms of spiritual energy. Remember, you are a physical being at the moment, even if spiritual at heart. It's important to honor and care for your body and nature at large. Alternatively, this card could be signaling a drought period of creative ideas, love, or fertility. How can you find small ways to work more creativity, love, and pleasure into your life to come back to the full energy of The Empress?

CARD 1

My focus
for the
month.

CARD 2

Roadblocks
I need to
overcome
this month.

CARD 3

Possibilities
that are in
store for me
this month.

What does this spread make me feel?

My takeaway for the month:

DECEMBER 2022

NOTES	SUNDAY	MONDAY	TUESDAY
	4	5	6
	11	12	13
	18	19	20
	25	26	27

18
HANUKKAH
(BEGINS AT SUNDOWN)

25
CHRISTMAS DAY

26
BOXING DAY
(UK / CAN / AUS / NZ)
KWANZAA

DECEMBER 2022

WEDNESDAY	THURSDAY	FRIDAY	SATURDAY
	1	2	3
	WORLD AIDS DAY		INTERNATIONAL DAY OF PERSONS WITH DISABILITIES
7	8	9	10
			HUMAN RIGHTS DAY
14	15	16	17
21	22	23	24
WINTER SOLSTICE			CHRISTMAS EVE
28	29	30	31
			NEW YEAR'S EVE

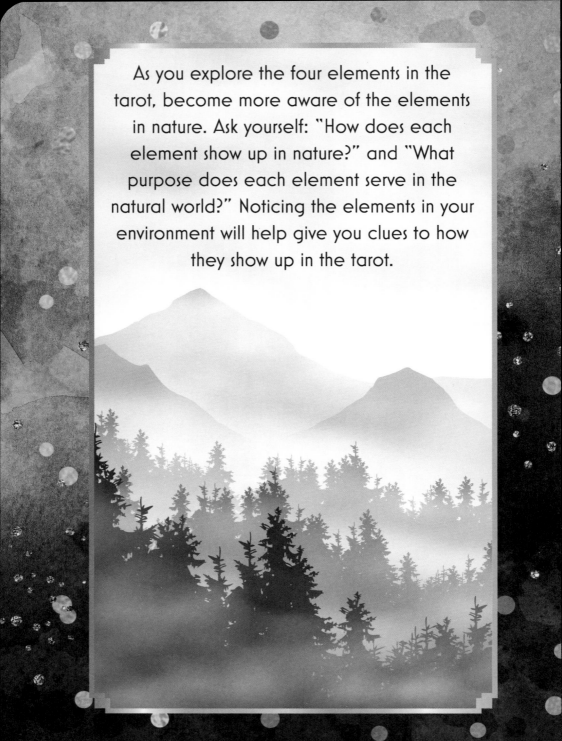

As you explore the four elements in the tarot, become more aware of the elements in nature. Ask yourself: "How does each element show up in nature?" and "What purpose does each element serve in the natural world?" Noticing the elements in your environment will help give you clues to how they show up in the tarot.

MONDAY (NOVEMBER) 28

TUESDAY (NOVEMBER) 29

WEDNESDAY (NOVEMBER) 30

THURSDAY 1
WORLD AIDS DAY

FRIDAY 2

SATURDAY 3
INTERNATIONAL DAY OF PERSONS WITH DISABILITIES

SUNDAY 4

DECEMBER 2022

MONDAY
5

TUESDAY
6

WEDNESDAY ●
7

THURSDAY
8

FRIDAY

9

SATURDAY

HUMAN RIGHTS DAY

10

SUNDAY

11

TWO OF WANDS
Everyone has goals. You have made some
progress towards yours. But there is still some
distance to go. Making plans for the next step
of your journey can help.

DECEMBER 2022

MONDAY 12

TUESDAY 13

WEDNESDAY 14

THURSDAY 15

FRIDAY  16

SATURDAY 17

SUNDAY 18
HANUKKAH (BEGINS AT SUNDOWN)

THREE OF PENTACLES
You have talents. But not everything you
have was secured on your own. You
had help along the way.

DECEMBER 2022

MONDAY 19

TUESDAY 20

WEDNESDAY 21
WINTER SOLSTICE

THURSDAY 22

FRIDAY ○

23

SATURDAY

CHRISTMAS EVE

24

SUNDAY

CHRISTMAS DAY

25

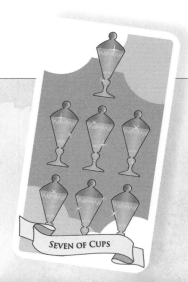

SEVEN OF CUPS

SEVEN OF CUPS

Choices! So many choices. But not all are equal. Some promised opportunities can be just what you are looking for. Others can be just pretty illusions. Look closely. Take your time. Try to see clearly.

JANUARY

THE EMPEROR

The Emperor represents divine masculine energy associated with leadership, power, and the ability to accomplish any goal. The energy of this card is stable and powerful. The zodiac sign associated with the Emperor is Aries, or the ram. The horns of the mighty ram indicate the ability to see any plan through to the end. Though the energy is fiery and intense, it is also stable and fatherly. The energy of the Emperor comes into your life to bring you strength and stability. If you're working diligently toward a goal, this card may appear to give you the strength you need to see it through. Alternatively, it may indicate a need to embody a more fatherly role in your life, bringing needed stability to you or those around you. It may benefit you to bring more structure into your life to accomplish your goals.

THE EMPEROR REVERSED

This card's reversed energy indicates that you may be overusing your force in ways that are causing harm to you or those around you. The fiery nature of this card can easily become addictive or turn into unhealthy workaholism. Alternatively, this reversed card could also indicate a total lack of power and a feeling of extreme vulnerability. If this is the case, what's something small you can do to feel more empowered?

CARD 1

My focus for the month.

CARD 2

Roadblocks I need to overcome this month.

CARD 3

Possibilities that are in store for me this month.

What does this spread make me feel?

My takeaway for the month:

JANUARY 2023

NOTES	SUNDAY	MONDAY	TUESDAY
	1 NEW YEAR'S DAY	2 BANK HOLIDAY (UK-SCT)	3
	8	9	10
	15	16 CIVIL RIGHTS DAY MARTIN LUTHER KING JR. DAY (US)	17
	22 CHINESE NEW YEAR	23	24
	29	30	31

JANUARY 2023

WEDNESDAY	THURSDAY	FRIDAY	SATURDAY
4	5 ●	6	7
11	12	13 ◗	14
18	19	20 ○	21
25	26 AUSTRALIA DAY	27 ◖ HOLOCAUST REMEMBRANCE DAY	28

Allow the depths of your emotions to flow.
Your internal oceans hold deep wisdom.

DECEMBER/JANUARY 2023

MONDAY (DECEMBER) 26
BOXING DAY (UK / CAN / AUS / NZ) / KWANZAA

TUESDAY (DECEMBER) 27

WEDNESDAY (DECEMBER) 28

THURSDAY (DECEMBER) 29

FRIDAY (DECEMBER) 30

SATURDAY (DECEMBER) 31
NEW YEAR'S EVE

SUNDAY 1
NEW YEAR'S DAY

JANUARY 2023

MONDAY
BANK HOLIDAY (UK–SCT)

2

TUESDAY

3

WEDNESDAY

4

THURSDAY

5

FRIDAY ● 6

SATURDAY 7

SUNDAY 8

NINE OF WANDS
Sometimes it seems like if it isn't one thing it
is another. You might feel as though your work
never ends or that others are arrayed against
you. But at the end of it all, you have what it
takes to succeed.

JANUARY 2023

MONDAY 9

TUESDAY 10

WEDNESDAY 11

THURSDAY 12

FRIDAY 13

SATURDAY 14

SUNDAY 15

ACE OF PENTACLES
A new opportunity has presented itself. This might be your chance to achieve what you have been striving for. How do you seize the moment? Are you willing to do what needs to be done?

JANUARY 2023

MONDAY
CIVIL RIGHTS DAY / MARTIN LUTHER KING JR. DAY (US)

16

TUESDAY

17

WEDNESDAY

18

THURSDAY

19

FRIDAY

20

SATURDAY ○

21

SUNDAY

22

CHINESE NEW YEAR

THREE OF CUPS

THREE OF CUPS

You are not alone. There are people in your life
to connect with—community, family, friends
new and old, maybe even an old enemy who
might have turned over a new leaf—or new
connections to make.

JANUARY 2023

MONDAY
23

TUESDAY
24

WEDNESDAY
25

THURSDAY
AUSTRALIA DAY
26

FRIDAY
HOLOCAUST REMEMBRANCE DAY

27

SATURDAY

28

SUNDAY

29

TEMPERANCE
There is a time to commit and a time to hang back. Where have you been putting your time and energy? Maybe now is a time to consider whether there is imbalance in your life. Remember, you are in this for the long haul!

FEBRUARY

THE HIEROPHANT

THE HIEROPHANT

This traditionally religious card is a call to seek out spiritual guidance for sources rooted in wisdom and deep knowledge. If organized religion speaks to you, you can go that route as well. If it doesn't, seek the ancestral wisdom you resonate with most. If you've been learning on your own in an area of your life, this card is calling you to pause and build a stronger foundation through someone who's gone before you. Ruled by stable Taurus, this card wants to know that you are infinite beyond belief, but there's no substitute for learning from those with more experience. This card could also indicate interactions with established structures.

THE HIEROPHANT REVERSED

When The Hierophant appears reversed, it could indicate you're unwilling to learn from others or have shut yourself off from deep wisdom. If this is the case, it will be in your best interest to find a teacher or source with which you feel more in line. Alternatively, the reversed nature of this card could indicate that you're being extremely rigid or arrogant in your beliefs and unwilling to look at any source of external knowledge. If this is the case, this card is calling you to let go of your stubbornness.

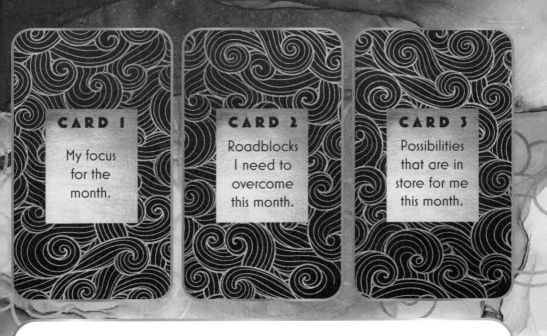

CARD 1

My focus for the month.

CARD 2

Roadblocks I need to overcome this month.

CARD 3

Possibilities that are in store for me this month.

What does this spread make me feel?

My takeaway for the month:

FEBRUARY 2023

NOTES	SUNDAY	MONDAY	TUESDAY
	● 5	6	7
	WAITANGI DAY (NZ)	WAITANGI DAY OBSERVED (NZ)	
	12	☽ 13	14
			VALENTINE'S DAY
	19	○ 20	21
		PRESIDENTS' DAY (US)	
	26	☽ 27	28

FEBRUARY 2023

WEDNESDAY	THURSDAY	FRIDAY	SATURDAY
1 FIRST DAY OF BLACK HISTORY MONTH	2 GROUNDHOG DAY (US / CAN)	3	4
8	9	10	11
15	16	17	18
22 ASH WEDNESDAY	23	24	25

Root yourself firmly into the present moment. The physical world is here to support you.

JANUARY/FEBRUARY 2023

MONDAY (JANUARY) 30

TUESDAY (JANUARY) 31

WEDNESDAY 1
FIRST DAY OF BLACK HISTORY MONTH

THURSDAY 2
GROUNDHOG DAY (US / CAN)

FRIDAY 3

SATURDAY 4

SUNDAY ● 5
WAITANGI DAY (NZ)

FEBRUARY 2023

MONDAY
WAITANGI DAY OBSERVED (NZ)

6

TUESDAY

7

WEDNESDAY

8

THURSDAY

9

FRIDAY

10

SATURDAY

11

SUNDAY

12

KNIGHT OF SWORDS
Confident in what you believe, you charge forward with conviction. Be certain about your course of action. Is that satisfaction from doing the right thing or simply doing? Look before you leap.

FEBRUARY 2023

MONDAY ☽

13

TUESDAY
VALENTINE'S DAY

14

WEDNESDAY

15

THURSDAY

16

FRIDAY   17

SATURDAY   18

SUNDAY   19

PAGE OF PENTACLES
There is much for you to learn. Contemplation
is your solace. Some might think you are
dreaming, but in fact you are planning and
growing. Just be sure to watch where you
are going.

FEBRUARY 2023

MONDAY ○
PRESIDENTS' DAY (US)

20

TUESDAY

21

WEDNESDAY
ASH WEDNESDAY

22

THURSDAY

23

FRIDAY 24

SATURDAY 25

SUNDAY 26

SEVEN OF WANDS
You have already come a long way. There is no possibility that you will turn back now. But are you feeling somewhat alone in your struggle? Or are others working against you? The odds might be long but are ultimately in your favor.

SEVEN OF WANDS

MARCH

THE LOVERS

THE LOVERS

THE LOVERS

Though this card can undoubtedly signal new love, partnership, or romance, the wisdom of The Lovers is much deeper than earthly relationships. It also signals a need to make an important decision. The decision you make will ultimately lead to more or less harmony in your life. Are there any important decisions looming in your life that could bring you closer to a place of balance and peace? The Lovers card is ruled by Gemini, and this airy sign often indicates a busy mind with many options at the ready. The Lovers calls you to sit with your options to find the best and most harmonious decision for you and those around you. The choices you make will likely have lasting effects far into the future. Listen to your higher self and trust your intuition.

THE LOVERS REVERSED

The reversed nature of this card could signal impending trouble in a relationship. It also asks you to reflect on any choices you've been putting off or neglecting. Alternatively, this card reversed could be trying to tell you that you're rushing a decision and moving too fast in an area of your life. Remember, the decision this card calls forth will have lasting effects on your life. Proceed with caution and take your time.

CARD 1

My focus
for the
month.

CARD 2

Roadblocks
I need to
overcome
this month.

CARD 3

Possibilities
that are in
store for me
this month.

What does this spread make me feel?

My takeaway for the month:

MARCH 2023

NOTES	SUNDAY	MONDAY	TUESDAY
	5	6	7
		PURIM (BEGINS AT SUNDOWN)	LABOUR DAY (AUS–ACT / NSW / SA)
	12	13	14
	DAYLIGHT SAVING TIME BEGINS (US / CAN)	LABOUR DAY (AUS–VIC)	
	19	20	21
	MOTHERING SUNDAY (UK)	SPRING EQUINOX	NOWRUZ
	26	27	28

MARCH 2023

WEDNESDAY	THURSDAY	FRIDAY	SATURDAY
1 FIRST DAY OF WOMEN'S HISTORY MONTH	2	3	4
8	9	10	11
☽ 15	16	17 ST. PATRICK'S DAY	18
22 RAMADAN (BEGINS AT SUNDOWN)	23	24	25
29	30	31	

Be open to new ways of being and seeing.
Inspiration from Spirit is all around.

FEBRUARY/MARCH 2023

MONDAY (FEBRUARY) ☽ 27

TUESDAY (FEBRUARY) 28

WEDNESDAY 1
FIRST DAY OF WOMEN'S HISTORY MONTH

THURSDAY 2

FRIDAY 3

SATURDAY 4

SUNDAY 5

MARCH 2023

MONDAY
PURIM (BEGINS AT SUNDOWN)

6

TUESDAY ●
LABOUR DAY (AUS-ACT / NSW / SA)

7

WEDNESDAY

8

THURSDAY

9

FRIDAY
10

SATURDAY
11

SUNDAY
12
DAYLIGHT SAVING TIME BEGINS (US / CAN)

NINE OF CUPS

Satisfaction is its own reward. Take stock of life and love. Find pleasure in what you have achieved. Indulge yourself. Relish what life has to offer you.

MARCH 2023

MONDAY
LABOUR DAY (AUS-VIC)
13

TUESDAY
14

WEDNESDAY ☽
15

THURSDAY
16

FRIDAY
ST. PATRICK'S DAY

17

SATURDAY

18

SUNDAY
MOTHERING SUNDAY (UK)

19

ACE OF SWORDS

ACE OF SWORDS
Shouting "Eureka!" may be going too far but
you could have just had or be on the verge of a
significant breakthrough. It may be a change in
your circumstances or a new understanding of
the world. In either case, savor it.

MARCH 2023

MONDAY
SPRING EQUINOX

20

TUESDAY ○
NOWRUZ

21

WEDNESDAY
RAMADAN (BEGINS AT SUNDOWN)

22

THURSDAY

23

FRIDAY

24

SATURDAY

25

SUNDAY

26

KNIGHT OF WANDS

You have what it takes to get things done. Let your enthusiasm and passion not only guide you but help you conquer your fears. But don't be careless! While your energy has power, make sure it takes you in the right direction.

APRIL

THE CHARIOT

The Chariot signals swift changes and a need to go with the flow. With The Lovers card we saw a call to make an important decision, and this card says that the wheels are in motion. The Chariot is ruled by watery and sensitive Cancer energy. These correspondences indicate that there's a deep need to flow with your emotions and not let yourself get caught up in them. Seek balance as you move forward, trusting that everything will work out in the end. You're always guided and surrounded by Spirit. As new experiences whirl into your world, greet them with grace and ease, then make a clear move. Dance through each new opportunity with clarity and deep trust that you have perfect control.

THE CHARIOT REVERSED

When The Chariot appears reversed, it often signals an inability to move forward. Due to the Cancer energy associated with this card, the feeling of being stuck likely has to do with your emotions. It's time to find a way to work through your emotions so you can move forward. Alternatively, the reversed expression of this card could be telling you that you've released control over your life and are wandering around aimlessly. It may be time to gain some clarity about your path.

CARD 1

My focus
for the
month.

CARD 2

Roadblocks
I need to
overcome
this month.

CARD 3

Possibilities
that are in
store for me
this month.

What does this spread make me feel?

My takeaway for the month:

APRIL 2023

NOTES	SUNDAY	MONDAY	TUESDAY
	2 PALM SUNDAY	3	4
	9 EASTER	10	11
	16 ORTHODOX EASTER	17 YOM HASHOAH (BEGINS AT SUNDOWN)	18
	23 30	24	25 ANZAC DAY (AUS / NZ)

APRIL 2023

WEDNESDAY	THURSDAY	FRIDAY	SATURDAY
			1 APRIL FOOLS' DAY
5 PASSOVER (BEGINS AT SUNDOWN)	6	7 GOOD FRIDAY	8
12	13	14	15
19	20	21 EID AL-FITR (BEGINS AT SUNDOWN)	22 EARTH DAY
26 ADMINISTRATIVE PROFESSIONALS' DAY (US)	27	28	29

Fan the flames of your internal fire;
the energy you need is you.

| MONDAY (MARCH) | 27 |

| TUESDAY (MARCH) | 28 |

| WEDNESDAY (MARCH) | 29 |

| THURSDAY (MARCH) | 30 |

| FRIDAY (MARCH) | 31 |

SATURDAY
APRIL FOOLS' DAY

1

SUNDAY
PALM SUNDAY

2

APRIL 2023

MONDAY
3

TUESDAY
4

WEDNESDAY
PASSOVER (BEGINS AT SUNDOWN)
5

THURSDAY
6

FRIDAY
GOOD FRIDAY

7

SATURDAY

8

SUNDAY
EASTER

9

FOUR OF PENTACLES
Once you have something you have long
desired, it is natural to want to keep it. But try
too hard and you might lose it. Protect what
you have. But do not forget to enjoy it as well.

APRIL 2023

MONDAY   10

TUESDAY   11

WEDNESDAY   12

THURSDAY ☽   13

FRIDAY
14

SATURDAY
15

SUNDAY
ORTHODOX EASTER
16

TEN OF CUPS
You might not have everything you want.
But do you have everything you need? Think
about what truly matters. It might be right in
front of you, or just around the corner.

APRIL 2023

MONDAY
YOM HASHOAH (BEGINS AT SUNDOWN)

17

TUESDAY

18

WEDNESDAY

19

THURSDAY ○

20

FRIDAY
EID AL-FITR (BEGINS AT SUNDOWN)

21

SATURDAY
EARTH DAY

22

SUNDAY

23

FIVE OF SWORDS
Confidence is ascendant in the aftermath of a victorious outcome. The field is yours. But things are not always that simple. Remember to avoid cockiness.

APRIL 2023

MONDAY
24

TUESDAY
ANZAC DAY (AUS / NZ)
25

WEDNESDAY
ADMINISTRATIVE PROFESSIONALS' DAY (US)
26

THURSDAY
27

FRIDAY

28

SATURDAY

29

SUNDAY

30

THE DEVIL

You will want to go deep inside to get to know your subconscious self, the one some call their shadow. What do you truly want or crave? Have there been times when those desires overwhelmed you? Or did you cause inner tension by limiting yourself?

MAY

STRENGTH

Strength comes in a variety of forms. Regardless of the form, when the Strength card presents, its energy has the power to change the world. This card calls you to be strong, and more importantly, to understand what strength looks like to you. Strength is ruled by the bold and bright sign of Leo. Leo reminds us to step into our power to inspire those around us. Are there areas where you've been holding yourself back? Now is the time to release any doubt or fears and let your voice be heard and your beauty seen. You're being called to face a situation with courage. This card also speaks to lust and carnal desires. Are there cravings that you've held yourself back from? Perhaps this card is calling you to face these desires head-on. Your strength, desires, and ability to shine are infinite.

STRENGTH REVERSED

This card's reversed nature implies that you may be avoiding something that you're scared to do or say. Strength is an important call to stand up for what is right and what you believe in. Even if your voice shakes, it's important to act in alignment with your soul. Trust that courage will be available when you need it. This card could also be referring to the misuse of strength. Be aware of how your desires could be negatively affecting you and those around you.

CARD 1

My focus for the month.

CARD 2

Roadblocks I need to overcome this month.

CARD 3

Possibilities that are in store for me this month.

What does this spread make me feel?

My takeaway for the month:

MAY 2023

NOTES	SUNDAY	MONDAY	TUESDAY
		1 LABOUR DAY (AUS-QLD) EARLY MAY BANK HOLIDAY (UK) FIRST DAY OF ASIAN AMERICAN AND PACIFIC ISLANDER HERITAGE MONTH	2
	7	8	9
	14 MOTHER'S DAY (US / CAN)	15	16
	21	22 VICTORIA DAY ((AN)	23
	28	29 SPRING BANK HOLIDAY (UK) MEMORIAL DAY (US)	30

MAY 2023

WEDNESDAY	THURSDAY	FRIDAY	SATURDAY
3	4	5	6
		CINCO DE MAYO	
10	11	12	13
17	18	19	20
24	25	26	27
31			

The fast-acting and communicative element of air comes to bring whispers and intuitive nudges of new beginnings. Air brings truth, inspiration, new ideas, and swift action.

MAY 2023

MONDAY
LABOUR DAY (AUS–QLD) / EARLY MAY BANK HOLIDAY (UK) /
FIRST DAY OF ASIAN AMERICAN AND PACIFIC ISLANDER HERITAGE MONTH

1

TUESDAY

2

WEDNESDAY

3

THURSDAY

4

FRIDAY ●
CINCO DE MAYO

5

SATURDAY

6

SUNDAY

7

MAY 2023

| MONDAY | 8 |

| TUESDAY | 9 |

| WEDNESDAY | 10 |

| THURSDAY | 11 |

FRIDAY

12

SATURDAY

13

SUNDAY
MOTHER'S DAY (US / CAN)

14

THREE OF WANDS

There are still more challenges to come. But
you are in a position of power and confidence.
You have good visibility for what is to come.
There is also the potential of finding a partner
who can help you achieve the kind of success
that you have long dreamed of.

THREE OF WANDS

MAY 2023

MONDAY 15

TUESDAY 16

WEDNESDAY 17

THURSDAY 18

FRIDAY ○   19

SATURDAY   20

SUNDAY   21

TEN OF WANDS
You might have been taking on too much.
Is there something weighing on you? This
may be a time to think about what you have
accomplished, the effort it took, and whether
you should have asked for help.

MAY 2023

MONDAY
VICTORIA DAY (CAN)

22

TUESDAY

23

WEDNESDAY

24

THURSDAY

25

FRIDAY   26

SATURDAY    27

SUNDAY   28

KING OF PENTACLES
Sometimes all of your hard work can have
a reward. Whether that is a material thing or
something as simple but as needed as some
space to relax, now could be the time to enjoy
what you have.

JUNE

THE HERMIT

The Hermit shows up to call you back to yourself. If you've been giving too much of your energy away, it's time to fill your own cup. Find a way to acknowledge your physical and spiritual needs in deeply fulfilling ways. When you take time to fill your mind, body, and soul, you'll find that the path ahead has always been lit to guide you on your way. If the light of your path dims, then it's time to retreat within again. The Hermit is ruled by practical and patient Virgo. The earthy energy of Virgo understands the importance of going within. This could be as simple as making time to get more organized or take care of things you've been putting off. Be open to the wisdom of Virgo and The Hermit to clean up any distractions that could be dimming your path.

THE HERMIT REVERSED

The reversed expression of this card signals that you may be avoiding time alone with yourself. If you've been in a phase of constant distractions, are the distractions still serving your highest good? Alternatively, Hermit energy to an extreme can manifest as an overabundance of caution and an inability to be around others. If this resonates with you, ask yourself what small things you could do to walk forward and trust that your path will be lit.

CARD 1

My focus for the month.

CARD 2

Roadblocks I need to overcome this month.

CARD 3

Possibilities that are in store for me this month.

What does this spread make me feel?

My takeaway for the month:

JUNE 2023

NOTES	SUNDAY	MONDAY	TUESDAY
	4	5	6
	11	12	13
	○ 18	19	20
	FATHER'S DAY (US / CAN / UK)	JUNETEENTH (US)	
	25 ☽	26	27

JUNE 2023

WEDNESDAY	THURSDAY	FRIDAY	SATURDAY
	1	2	3
	FIRST DAY OF PRIDE MONTH		
7	8	9	10
14	15	16	17
FLAG DAY (US)			
21	22	23	24
SUMMER SOLSTICE			
28	29	30	

When you find yourself digging deep for the inner resources to carry on, the element of fire comes to help you complete the task at hand.

MAY/JUNE 2023

MONDAY (MAY)
SPRING BANK HOLIDAY (UK) / MEMORIAL DAY (US)

29

TUESDAY (MAY)

30

WEDNESDAY (MAY)

31

THURSDAY
FIRST DAY OF PRIDE MONTH

1

FRIDAY

2

SATURDAY ●

3

SUNDAY

4

JUNE 2023

MONDAY
5

TUESDAY
6

WEDNESDAY
7

THURSDAY
8

FRIDAY

9

SATURDAY ☽

10

SUNDAY

11

EIGHT OF CUPS
Not every victory is easily earned. There
are setbacks in your journey. These can be
cause for concern or a reason to recoup. Give
yourself more chances. Do not be afraid to try
a different path or ask for directions.

JUNE 2023

MONDAY   12

TUESDAY   13

WEDNESDAY   14
FLAG DAY (US)

THURSDAY   15

FRIDAY

16

SATURDAY

17

SUNDAY ○

18

FATHER'S DAY (US / CAN / UK)

THREE OF SWORDS
Loss and pain are unavoidable. They are also
not permanent. Do not avoid what happened
to you. Facing your hurt can bring it down to
size and maybe even make the next time easier
to bear.

THREE OF SWORDS

JUNE 2023

MONDAY.
JUNETEENTH HOLIDAY

19

TUESDAY

20

WEDNESDAY
SUMMER SOLSTICE

21

THURSDAY

22

FRIDAY

23

SATURDAY

24

SUNDAY

25

QUEEN OF WANDS

Your confidence is an asset, as is your luck.
Charm, magnetism, and optimism bring others
into your orbit. Listen to your nurturing side.
Be careful not to give too much.

THE WHEEL OF FORTUNE

This potent card comes up as a reminder to find a point of stillness amid the constant changes life offers. The wheel of life, much like the cycles of the Moon, is always moving. Even in our darkest moments, life must go on. This doesn't mean that we can't find peace or seek respite during the more turbulent phases. It does mean that our efforts to prevent difficult things from happening likely won't work. The Wheel of Fortune often indicates a time of great expansion, which could signal growth into a new phase or cycle of life. This card corresponds with the planet Jupiter, which signals a time of growth and possible good fortunes. If you've found yourself in a tumultuous time, this card can also appear as a reminder that nothing is permanent. An opportunity to excel may be just around the corner.

THE WHEEL OF FORTUNE REVERSED

When this card appears reversed, it can indicate that you're pushing against the natural flow of the Universe or are unwilling to accept changes. Trying to force a phase may backfire and will keep you from growing toward the best version of yourself. This card reversal may also indicate that your luck could be taking a turn for the worse. If this is the case, know that it's only temporary.

CARD 1

My focus for the month.

CARD 2

Roadblocks I need to overcome this month.

CARD 3

Possibilities that are in store for me this month.

What does this spread make me feel?

My takeaway for the month:

JULY 2023

NOTES	SUNDAY	MONDAY	TUESDAY
	2 ●	3	4 INDEPENDENCE DAY (US)
	◗ 9	10	11
	16 ○	17	18
	23	24 ◖	25
	30	31	

JULY 2023

WEDNESDAY	THURSDAY	FRIDAY	SATURDAY
			1 CANADA DAY (CAN)
5	6	7	8
12	13	14	15
19	20	21	22
26	27	28	29

You have free will and will always have free will. The cards are not your fate.

MONDAY (JUNE) 26

TUESDAY (JUNE) 27

WEDNESDAY (JUNE) 28

THURSDAY (JUNE) 29

FRIDAY (JUNE) 30

SATURDAY 1
CANADA DAY (CAN)

SUNDAY 2

JULY 2023

MONDAY ●   3

TUESDAY   4
INDEPENDENCE DAY (US)

WEDNESDAY   5

THURSDAY   6

FRIDAY

7

SATURDAY

8

SUNDAY ◗

9

SIX OF PENTACLES
Have you come into some good fortune? If so, spread the wealth! Nothing shows your appreciation for everything you have been given like giving to others.

JULY 2023

MONDAY 10

TUESDAY 11

WEDNESDAY 12

THURSDAY 13

FRIDAY

14

SATURDAY

15

SUNDAY

16

PAGE OF CUPS
Inspiration is like lightning, only not as
dangerous (usually). It cannot be planned, it
makes your hair stand up, and afterward you
might look at things differently.

PAGE OF CUPS

JULY 2023

MONDAY ○   17

TUESDAY   18

WEDNESDAY   19

THURSDAY   20

FRIDAY

21

SATURDAY

22

SUNDAY

23

FOUR OF SWORDS

While a good defense can be a good offense,
sometimes an even better defense is doing
nothing at all. Pulling back from the world is
a perfectly fine reaction to tough times. Seek
rest and recovery so that when you return you
are prepared.

JULY 2023

MONDAY   24

TUESDAY ◖   25

WEDNESDAY   26

THURSDAY   27

FRIDAY   28

SATURDAY   29

SUNDAY   30

THE TOWER
Sudden disruption may be on the way. What
kind of upheavals have you had recently? How
did you bounce back? Draw on that strength
to face the change that is coming without fear
or hesitation.

AUGUST

JUSTICE

Justice can appear in your reading for a variety of reasons. The nature of this card is rooted in a deep need for truth. Truth is divine, and truth cannot exist without justice. Justice and equality are written into the fabric of our Universe and will always come to be eventually. This card could be showing up as a good omen in a legal situation, if you are in the right. If you are not in the right, this is your call to do what needs to be done to ensure that you're aligned with truth and the highest good for all. This card is ruled by the harmony-seeking sign of Libra. Libra will always strive to strike a perfect balance to please themselves and those around them. On a more personal level, this card may be an invitation to explore your balance, or lack of balance, in relationships with others. On the other hand, you may need to open yourself up more to receiving love and kindness from others. Be open to exploring where you can be in better balance with those you interact with.

JUSTICE REVERSED

This card's reversed expression calls you to assess where in your life you've been unjust or caused harm. If this is the case, take steps to clean up your side of the street and make impactful amends. This card reversed could also indicate an imbalance in your life. Be honest with yourself about areas that may be out of sync and what you can do to have more balance in your life.

CARD 1

My focus for the month.

CARD 2

Roadblocks I need to overcome this month.

CARD 3

Possibilities that are in store for me this month.

What does this spread make me feel?

My takeaway for the month:

AUGUST 2023

NOTES	SUNDAY	MONDAY	TUESDAY
			1
	6	7	8
	13	14	15
	20	21	22
	27	28	29

SUMMER BANK HOLIDAY
(UK-ENG / NIR / WAL)

AUGUST 2023

WEDNESDAY	THURSDAY	FRIDAY	SATURDAY
2	3	4	5
9	10	11	12
○ 16	17	18	19
23 ☽	24	25	26
● 30	31		

To achieve a deeper personal understanding, journal about the cards that make you the most uncomfortable.

JULY/AUGUST 2023

MONDAY (JULY)	31
TUESDAY ●	1
WEDNESDAY	2
THURSDAY	3
FRIDAY	4
SATURDAY	5
SUNDAY	6

AUGUST 2023

MONDAY   7

TUESDAY ☽   8

WEDNESDAY   9

THURSDAY   10

FRIDAY   11

SATURDAY   12

SUNDAY   13

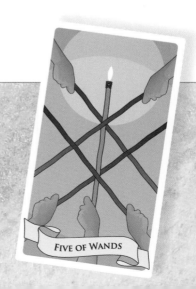

FIVE OF WANDS
Do not seek them out, but be aware of
the conflict and dissent in your life. These
struggles can be highly disruptive but can also
be a source of renewal. Look for lessons in the
strife. See what you can learn.

AUGUST 2023

MONDAY   14

TUESDAY   15

WEDNESDAY ○   16

THURSDAY   17

FRIDAY

18

SATURDAY

19

SUNDAY

20

KNIGHT OF PENTACLES

All work and no play may not sound good, but
it can be satisfying. You are steady, responsible.
Predictable? Sometimes. But trustworthy. Do
not forget: your efforts have a purpose.

AUGUST 2023

MONDAY 21

TUESDAY 22

WEDNESDAY 23

THURSDAY 24

FRIDAY   25

SATURDAY   26

SUNDAY   27

FOUR OF CUPS
Jumping at every chance offered you is not just
bad planning, it's exhausting. But this may not
last. Take advantage while you can.

SEPTEMBER

THE HANGED MAN

THE HANGED MAN

THE HANGED ONE

Receiving this card may indicate that it's time to sink into acceptance around a current situation. If you've found yourself pushing or fighting against something, this is your call to stop. The Hanged One calls you to try a different vantage point and be okay with doing nothing for a while. If you're stuck in a place of trying to force a situation, the answer can often be found in releasing and letting go of what you thought needed to be done. In your place of stillness, you may find that new ideas or the perfect answer come to you with little to no effort. This card is ruled by the planet Neptune, the king of the sea. The watery and intuitive energy associated with this card implies a need for spiritual connection. Trust that whatever you need will come with little to no force on your part.

THE HANGED ONE REVERSED

The reversed energy of this card suggests that you might be unwilling to let go of a situation. If you've been trying to force something to happen and there's no sign of it changing, this is a plea to let it go. Alternatively, this card's extreme reversed expression indicates that you've gone too far out into a dreamworld and are out of touch with reality.

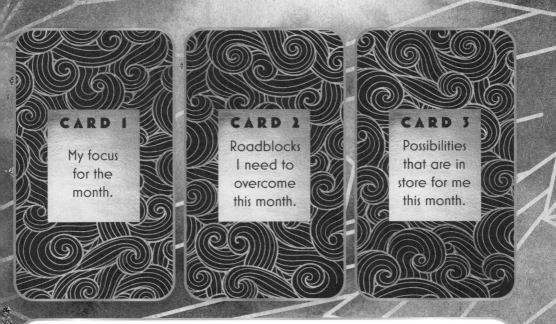

CARD 1

My focus for the month.

CARD 2

Roadblocks I need to overcome this month.

CARD 3

Possibilities that are in store for me this month.

What does this spread make me feel?

My takeaway for the month:

SEPTEMBER 2023

NOTES	SUNDAY	MONDAY	TUESDAY
	3	4	5
	FATHER'S DAY (AUS / NZ)	LABOR DAY (US) LABOUR DAY (CAN)	
	10	11	12
	GRANDPARENTS' DAY (US)	PATRIOT DAY (US)	
	17	18	19
	24	25	26
	YOM KIPPUR (BEGINS AT SUNDOWN)		

SEPTEMBER 2023

WEDNESDAY	THURSDAY	FRIDAY	SATURDAY
		1	2
6	7	8	9
13	14	15	16
		ROSH HASHANAH (BEGINS AT SUNDOWN) FIRST DAY OF NATIONAL HISPANIC HERITAGE MONTH	
20	21	22	23
			FALL EQUINOX
27	28	29	30
		SUKKOT (BEGINS AT SUNDOWN)	

To enhance your readings, work with crystals that inspire intuition, like amethyst, labradorite, and kyanite.

AUGUST/SEPTEMBER 2023

MONDAY (AUGUST) 28
SUMMER BANK HOLIDAY (UK-ENG / NIR / WAL)

TUESDAY (AUGUST) 29

WEDNESDAY (AUGUST) ● 30

THURSDAY (AUGUST) 31

FRIDAY 1

SATURDAY 2

SUNDAY 3
FATHER'S DAY (AUS / NZ)

SEPTEMBER 2023

MONDAY
LABOR DAY (US) / LABOUR DAY (CAN)

4

TUESDAY

5

WEDNESDAY ☽

6

THURSDAY

7

FRIDAY
8

SATURDAY
9

SUNDAY
GRANDPARENTS' DAY (US)
10

SIX OF SWORDS
The process of changing from one state of being or environment to another may cause friction. But you can also see it as a good time to let go of the burdens of your past. Face the future clearly, honestly, and positively.

SEPTEMBER 2023

MONDAY
PATRIOT DAY (US)

11

TUESDAY

12

WEDNESDAY

13

THURSDAY ○

14

FRIDAY

ROSH HASHANAH (BEGINS AT SUNDOWN) /
FIRST DAY OF NATIONAL HISPANIC HERITAGE MONTH

15

SATURDAY

16

SUNDAY

17

PAGE OF WANDS

Ah, to be young and unbound by cynicism or fear. Be open to that which is new and exciting. Recall the thrill that courses through you when you are about to set off on an adventure. The tension and uncertainty, as well. It is all part of the process of renewal.

SEPTEMBER 2023

MONDAY	18

TUESDAY	19

WEDNESDAY	20

THURSDAY	21

FRIDAY

22

SATURDAY
FALL EQUINOX

23

SUNDAY
YOM KIPPUR (BEGINS AT SUNDOWN)

24

SEVEN OF PENTACLES

Pausing, in work or in your journey, gives you
an opportunity for rest. It can also provide
a chance for reassessment. What are you
laboring for, after all? Are you headed in the
right direction? Maybe it is time to check
that map.

SEVEN OF PENTACLES

OCTOBER

THE MOON

The Moon card beckons you inward and asks you to explore your internal shadows. Shadow work is the act of making a conscious effort to explore your fears and repressed emotions; it's through performing this work that you become whole. The Moon card is your reminder to honor all facets of yourself. Be cautiously curious of new people or influences that come into your life and take time to get clear on their motives. It will be important for you to connect within before making any decisions. This card may also be calling you to connect to the energy of the Moon. The Moon has long been associated with the Divine Feminine, intuition, cycles, and the passage of time. Deep inner work requires a certain passivity and softness often associated with femininity. Be gentle with yourself as you embark on any shadow work.

THE MOON REVERSED

The reversed Moon card signifies a possible unveiling of confusion that may be on the horizon. Disorientating situations will begin to make more sense or clear up. People around you may open up about situations that once escaped you. The reversed Moon could indicate that fear, anxiety, or confusion has taken hold of you. It also calls you close to reveal any stuck emotions that have become habit energy in your inner world. Lastly, if you've neglected your intuitive gifts, the reversed Moon may be asking you to explore them.

CARD 1

My focus for the month.

CARD 2

Roadblocks I need to overcome this month.

CARD 3

Possibilities that are in store for me this month.

What does this spread make me feel?

My takeaway for the month:

OCTOBER 2023

NOTES	SUNDAY	MONDAY	TUESDAY
	1	2	3
		LABOUR DAY (AUS-ACT / NSW / SA)	
	8	9	10
		INDIGENOUS PEOPLES' DAY (US) COLUMBUS DAY (US) THANKSGIVING DAY (CAN)	
	15	16	17
	22	23	24
		LABOUR DAY (NZ)	
	29	30	31
			HALLOWEEN

OCTOBER 2023

WEDNESDAY	THURSDAY	FRIDAY	SATURDAY
4	5	6	7
			SIMCHAT TORAH (BEGINS AT SUNDOWN)
11	12	13	14
18	19	20	21
25	26	27	28

At a loss on what to ask the cards? Try asking these questions:
How can I inspire spiritual growth? What is my biggest soul
lesson? Where will I find the most joy? How can I best honor
my journey? How can I best share my gifts with others? What is
my primary purpose during my journey?

SEPTEMBER/OCTOBER 2023

MONDAY (SEPTEMBER)   25

TUESDAY (SEPTEMBER)   26

WEDNESDAY (SEPTEMBER)   27

THURSDAY (SEPTEMBER)   28

FRIDAY (SEPTEMBER) ●   29
SUKKOT (BEGINS AT SUNDOWN)

SATURDAY (SEPTEMBER)   30

SUNDAY   1

OCTOBER 2023

MONDAY
LABOUR DAY (AUS-ACT / NSW / SA)

2

TUESDAY

3

WEDNESDAY

4

THURSDAY

5

FRIDAY ☽

6

SATURDAY
SIMCHAT TORAH (BEGINS AT SUNDOWN)

7

SUNDAY

8

KING OF CUPS

KING OF CUPS
Maintain your balance. Rise above squabbles
and negativity. Do not inhibit your feelings
but direct them. Other people respect your
even-handedness and wisdom. They will want
your advice.

OCTOBER 2023

MONDAY
INDIGENOUS PEOPLES' DAY (US) / COLUMBUS DAY (US) / THANKSGIVING DAY (CAN)

9

TUESDAY

10

WEDNESDAY

11

THURSDAY

12

FRIDAY 13

SATURDAY ○ 14

SUNDAY 15

SEVEN OF SWORDS

Honesty is always the best policy. Except
when it's not. There are times when stealth is
the better option. But not everybody is going
to agree with that. Just be ready for what may
come afterwards.

SEVEN OF SWORDS

OCTOBER 2023

MONDAY 16

TUESDAY 17

WEDNESDAY 18

THURSDAY 19

FRIDAY

20

SATURDAY

21

SUNDAY

22

SIX OF WANDS
Things are not perfect. But you have been able to marshal your skills and meet your goal. This could be a time to bask in your success.

OCTOBER 2023

MONDAY
LABOUR DAY (NZ)

23

TUESDAY

24

WEDNESDAY

25

THURSDAY

26

FRIDAY   27

SATURDAY ●   28

SUNDAY   29

JUDGEMENT
For every action there is a reaction. Have you
been wronged by someone? Have you yourself
wronged someone? Examine the past and
determine how you will move into the future,
free of burdens and judgements.

NOVEMBER

THE STAR

The bright light of The Star comes in after the intensity of The Tower. This card appears to offer hope and inspiration. It's safe to believe that you are here for a purpose. The divine guidance and hope of The Star is not something outside of you but rather a force that dwells deep within. This is an energy you can turn to anytime you need to be inspired and renewed. The Star is ruled by the sign of Aquarius. Aquarius energy loves to stand out, is a freethinker, and believes in the good of others. This card's Aquarian energy calls you to believe in yourself and present yourself in the world as authentically as possible. Anytime you lose sight of your path, go within to connect with the divine wisdom of your inner light.

THE STAR REVERSED

When The Star shows up reversed, it may indicate that you're having difficulty seeing a way through. You may be experiencing a time of lost hope and believe that your life is doomed to failure. If you've faced many hardships, it can feel extremely vulnerable to have hope. Having hope means you might fail. However, if you never allow yourself to envision a brighter future, you'll never know the path to get there. This card reversed calls you to face your vulnerability around hoping for better and to find ways to see the good around you.

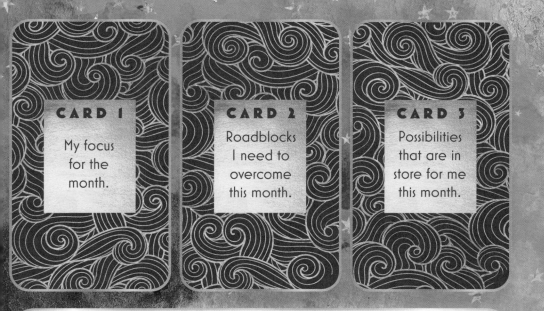

CARD 1

My focus for the month.

CARD 2

Roadblocks I need to overcome this month.

CARD 3

Possibilities that are in store for me this month.

What does this spread make me feel?

My takeaway for the month:

NOVEMBER 2023

NOTES	SUNDAY	MONDAY	TUESDAY
	5	6	7
	DAYLIGHT SAVING TIME ENDS (US / CAN)		ELECTION DAY (US)
	12	13	14
	19	20	21
	26	27	28

NOVEMBER 2023

WEDNESDAY	THURSDAY	FRIDAY	SATURDAY
1 ALL SAINTS' DAY	2	3	4
8	9	10	11 VETERANS DAY (US)
15	16	17	18
22	23 THANKSGIVING DAY (US)	24 NATIVE AMERICAN HERITAGE DAY (US)	25
29	30		

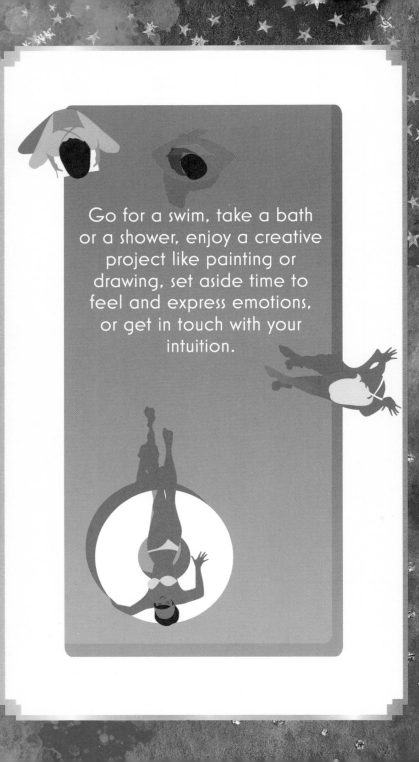

Go for a swim, take a bath or a shower, enjoy a creative project like painting or drawing, set aside time to feel and express emotions, or get in touch with your intuition.

OCTOBER/NOVEMBER 2023

MONDAY (OCTOBER)
30

TUESDAY (OCTOBER)
HALLOWEEN
31

WEDNESDAY
ALL SAINTS' DAY
1

THURSDAY
2

FRIDAY
3

SATURDAY
4

SUNDAY ☽
DAYLIGHT SAVING TIME ENDS (US / CAN)
5

NOVEMBER 2023

MONDAY
6

TUESDAY
ELECTION DAY (US)
7

WEDNESDAY
8

THURSDAY
9

FRIDAY   10

SATURDAY   11
VETERANS DAY (US)

SUNDAY   12

TEN OF PENTACLES
Good things will come. Maybe they have
already. Is it time to look back at what you
have done, what you have gained? It could
be wealth, family, or something else rare
and wonderful.

NOVEMBER 2023

MONDAY ○   13

TUESDAY   14

WEDNESDAY   15

THURSDAY   16

FRIDAY

17

SATURDAY

18

SUNDAY

19

SIX OF CUPS
The past is in the past, but it never disappears. Are you returning to a familiar place with strong associations? Is there a memory you cannot shake? There might be a sensation, a discovery, or even a person from earlier in your life that is worth revisiting.

NOVEMBER 2023

MONDAY ☽   20

TUESDAY   21

WEDNESDAY   22

THURSDAY   23
THANKSGIVING DAY (US)

FRIDAY
NATIVE AMERICAN HERITAGE DAY (US)

24

SATURDAY

25

SUNDAY

26

QUEEN OF SWORDS
Strength can be perceived as harshness, but it does not have to be. What you have learned and gone through has given you wisdom, as well as independence, and a strong set of principles. Use all those gifts to answer the questions you are being asked.

DECEMBER

THE SUN

The Sun card is always a welcome sight. This card calls you to play and enjoy the bounty of life around you. Call to mind the areas of your life that inspire the most joy and allow yourself to stay there for a moment. If you never allow yourself time to celebrate the happiest moments of life, they'll slip through your fingers, as all time does. Sometimes it's important to create your own joy in life. If you've gone through a difficult time or are in the midst of one now, how can you bring a little light from the sun into your life? Cultivate a childlike curiosity when it comes to embracing happiness. The Sun card also signals an abundance of health and vibrancy. It may be arriving to signal you to take action and enjoy this extra burst of energy.

THE SUN REVERSED

The reversed expression of this card indicates that you're cutting yourself off from experiencing joy. Have you caught yourself in a cycle of always seeing the glass half empty? This card is asking you to observe whether or not your denial of happiness is serving you. This card could also indicate a need to get in touch with your inner child. Perhaps there's part of your youth that needs some healing, or you just need to find more ways to invite play into your life.

CARD 1

My focus for the month.

CARD 2

Roadblocks I need to overcome this month.

CARD 3

Possibilities that are in store for me this month.

What does this spread make me feel?

My takeaway for the month:

DECEMBER 2023

NOTES	SUNDAY	MONDAY	TUESDAY
	3	4	5
	INTERNATIONAL DAY OF PERSONS WITH DISABILITIES		
	10	11	12
	HUMAN RIGHTS DAY		
	17	18	19
	24	25	26
	CHRISTMAS EVE		
	31		BOXING DAY (UK / CAN / AUS / NZ)
	NEW YEAR'S EVE	CHRISTMAS DAY	KWANZAA

DECEMBER 2023

WEDNESDAY	THURSDAY	FRIDAY	SATURDAY
		1 WORLD AIDS DAY	2
6	7 HANUKKAH (BEGINS AT SUNDOWN)	8	9
13	14	15	16
20	21 WINTER SOLSTICE	22	23
27	28	29	30

Go for a walk in nature, meditate sitting
on the earth, garden, exercise, or
prepare a meal for yourself from scratch.

NOVEMBER/DECEMBER 2023

MONDAY (NOVEMBER) ●	27
TUESDAY (NOVEMBER)	28
WEDNESDAY (NOVEMBER)	29
THURSDAY (NOVEMBER)	30
FRIDAY WORLD AIDS DAY	1
SATURDAY	2
SUNDAY INTERNATIONAL DAY OF PERSONS WITH DISABILITIES	3

DECEMBER 2023

MONDAY   4

TUESDAY ☽   5

WEDNESDAY   6

THURSDAY   7
HANUKKAH (BEGINS AT SUNDOWN)

FRIDAY

8

SATURDAY

9

SUNDAY
HUMAN RIGHTS DAY

10

EIGHT OF WANDS

Things are in motion but in what direction and to what end it is more difficult to say. What do your other cards tell you? It could be time to get on the move. Take hold of that energy and use it to your advantage.

DECEMBER 2023

MONDAY   11

TUESDAY   12

○

WEDNESDAY   13

THURSDAY   14

FRIDAY
15

SATURDAY
16

SUNDAY
17

NINE OF PENTACLES
Prosperity and achievement might be in
your grasp. You have something to celebrate.
Are you solitary in this state or is that
independence? Learn to luxuriate.

DECEMBER 2023

MONDAY 18

TUESDAY 19

WEDNESDAY 20

THURSDAY 21
WINTER SOLSTICE

FRIDAY

22

SATURDAY

23

SUNDAY
CHRISTMAS EVE

24

QUEEN OF CUPS
Intuition and empathy are your guides.
Sometimes you can tell what others need
before they do. Other times you are searching
for counsel of your own.

DECEMBER 2023

MONDAY
CHRISTMAS DAY

25

TUESDAY
BOXING DAY (UK / CAN / AUS / NZ) / KWANZAA

26

WEDNESDAY

27

THURSDAY

28

FRIDAY

29

SATURDAY

30

SUNDAY
NEW YEAR'S EVE

31

KING OF WANDS

There is a leader within you. When you point the way, others trust and follow. But what is your vision? Where are you taking them or yourself? Make a plan and be a success.

NOTES

NOTES

Brimming with creative inspiration, how-to projects, and useful information to enrich your everyday life, quarto.com is a favorite destination for those pursuing their interests and passions.

© 2022 by Quarto Publishing Group USA Inc.
Text © 2021 by Cassie Uhl

First published in 2022 by Rock Point, an imprint of The Quarto Group,
142 West 36th Street, 4th Floor, New York, NY 10018, USA
T (212) 779-4972 F (212) 779-6058 www.Quarto.com

Contains content previously published in 2021 as *The Zenned Out Guide to Understanding Tarot* by Rock Point, an imprint of The Quarto Group, 142 West 36th Street, 4th Floor, New York, NY 10018

Rock Point titles are also available at discount for retail, wholesale, promotional, and bulk purchase. For details, contact the Special Sales Manager by email at specialsales@quarto.com or by mail at The Quarto Group, Attn: Special Sales Manager, 100 Cummings Center Suite 265D, Beverly, MA 01915 USA.

10 9 8 7 6 5 4 3 2 1

ISBN: 978-1-63106-893-5

Publisher: Rage Kindelsperger
Creative Director: Laura Drew
Managing Editor: Cara Donaldson
Project Editor: Sara Bonacum
Cover and Interior Design: Beth Middleworth

Printed in China

This planner provides general information on tarot and positive spiritual habits. However, it should not be relied upon as recommending or promoting any specific diagnosis or method of treatment for a particular condition, and it is not intended as a substitute for medical advice or for direct diagnosis and treatment of a medical condition by a qualified physician. Readers who have questions about a particular condition, possible treatments for that condition, or possible reactions from the condition or its treatment should consult a physician or other qualified healthcare professional.

All moon phases shown are for the Eastern Time Zone.